Woman at t

Reflections on the story of Jesus a

By: Melissa Calloway

Dedication

To God for waiting at my well

Introduction

My first book, "The Proverbs 31 Project", revolved around the nearly perfect and noble woman of Proverbs 31. While this woman is one of the most inspiring characters of the Bible, I think a lot of us can confidently admit that we are thinking, *Girl, you need to chill. Also, quit making our husbands think that we will run a vineyard and clothing line with 4 kids, and that he will never hear us burp or snore.* Enter the Samaritan woman from the Book of John. I wouldn't say she is the complete opposite of the Proverbs 31 woman, but she is definitely in a different category. I'm also not saying that one category is better than another. That is why I want to use this opportunity to take a deeper exploration of the exchange between Jesus and her.

This conversation, in my opinion, is one of the most impactful scriptures in all the books of the Bible. Although it was a brief encounter, the depth could be measured in miles. I honestly can't tell you how many times I've read this part of scripture, but what Jesus is teaching here didn't exactly hit me until around the 86th time. I took away five very valuable lessons: 1) Jesus interrupts us in daily routines, especially when we are going through the motions; 2) He crosses all barriers, showing no favor to one particular type of person; 3) He teaches that surrender is the first step within salvation, which is not as easy as it sounds; 4) He teaches us how to pray, and 5) He wants us to share His life with others.

Now let's dive into the discussion between Jesus and the Samaritan woman. In fact, as you read the Word, don't just see Jesus with this Samaritan woman. Imagine you are at the well with Jesus, that He was waiting for you to arrive. Let Him speak to you, and ask yourself at the end of this book, if Jesus offered me what He was offering to this woman, how would I respond?

Going Through the Motions

Jesus had to go through Samaria on the way. Eventually He came to the Samaritan village of Sychar, near the field that Jacob gave to his son, Joseph. Jacob's well was there; and Jesus, tired from the long walk, sat wearily beside the well about noontime. Soon a Samaritan woman came to draw water, and Jesus said to her, "Please give me a drink". He was alone at the time, because His disciples had gone into the village to buy some food. (John 4:4-8)

As we read the scripture above, we see a Samaritan woman going to Jacob's Well to retrieve water. At first, this encounter may seem like a coincidence. Jesus is simply asking a random woman for some water, because He has been traveling by foot for many miles. This is not the case. Everything Jesus did was on purpose. Have you ever been in the middle of something and felt the need to pray? Maybe something happened in the middle of a mediocre day, and now God is all you can think about? When was the last time you encountered Jesus?

After I read this conversation a few times, I realized it represented what waiting looks like when we are going through the motions. Sometimes when we are waiting for fulfillment in some area of our lives, we try to find ways to solve this problem without seeking God first. We look for earthly answers, which can also be seen as temporary fixes (which we never realize are temporary until they just go poof! Can I get an *"Amen"*?) We look for quick fixes, but most of the time, our poor decision-making skills cause us to possibly feel emptiness, apathy, regret, and/or other negative feelings. For example, we use gluttony, alcohol, drugs, toxic relationships, and other unhealthy habits to find some temporary relief, but what we're really waiting for is lasting peace.

Most of us have a routine. Whether you are single, married, divorced, have children, have pets, in school, working through medical concerns, organizing extracurricular obligations, etc., all of us can admit that we try, for sanity purposes, to have a routine. We have organizers, planners, calendars, and sometimes we even hire people to tell us what our schedule is and/or live our routine alongside us. However, I have a question. When was the last time you let yourself sit down in the midst of chaos, close your eyes, take a deep breath in and exhale slowly? Maybe some of you are telling me that kind of behavior can be irresponsible, especially if you are late for work or trying to calm down 3 crying children. I totally get it. All of us have responsibilities and timelines, but are you just going through the motions of life? Are you in robot mode for a few years, waiting for another period of your life to begin something you want?

There is a certain priority with everything on our daily to-do list; otherwise, those tasks wouldn't be there. There are needs that are more urgent than others, like feeding the baby over folding laundry. We know it all needs to get done eventually. Jesus did something interesting here in the scripture; in the middle of the woman's task, He asked her for a drink of water. He asked her to stop her task to give Him attention. If we look at spending time with God as a task, then we will feel overwhelmed. Spending time with God is not about a checkbox though. God is our Father, and just like you want to spend time with your significant other, friends, family, and/or children, Jesus wants us to want to spend time with Him. He doesn't want to be an obligation. It's kind of funny when you think about it, because I'm guilty of saying this and I've heard others say similar things: "*I don't have time to sit and read the Bible, because I have to cook, clean, study, work out, finish spreadsheets, blah blah blah*". Everything we're doing is for Him though. The whole reason we are walking on this Earth is because of Him. He gave you that job, those children, that home, and your body. To say He doesn't fit in, well darling, He's all of it. God doesn't condemn us for not spending time with Him, nor does He expect us to talk to Him for hours non-stop. All that being said, there is no section of your life that Jesus doesn't fit into. If there is, that is where He will meet you.

This leads me to an unexpected interruption I had during an extremely difficult time in my life. At first, I thought it was from the depths of hell, because it was regarding the DMV (Department of Motor Vehicles). Before I continue, I just want to say that if you work at a DMV, I am sure you are a wonderful person; my experience was extremely dramatic because of the additional stressors in my life. This is not a standard story.

During an extremely tough season of my life, I was required to travel, and as many of us know, traveling is rarely simple. After I packed my luggage, I checked my purse for my license. It was then I noticed that my card was going to expire in three days, which was also celebrated in previous years as my birthday. Yes, I had to go to the DMV on my birthday, but I'll get to that in a second. Through my blurred vision from all the crying, I read the DMV website on what I needed to take with me and went first thing on Monday, since I realized this on a weekend. I waited in line for over an hour, and when I got to the counter, she said that I needed an additional piece of mail to prove I was a resident.

I'm not going to lie. I looked rough. I had huge circles under my eyes, no make-up, and was wearing an oversized hoodie, jeans, and old sneakers. I didn't look like I really had it together, but I was confident on what I read on the website. To avoid a huge meltdown, I asked her what I needed to grab from my house and said that I would be right back. (That really meant an hour later.) I waited in line for another hour and a half. A new lady was at the counter, and when I gave her my 16 inch folder of all the documents I needed to get a new license, she told me I was missing another document. She said that my registration wasn't completely there. I remember feeling the tears start to well up in my eyes. As much as I could, yet with a very shaky voice, I explained to her that I was here earlier that morning and another woman told me that all the documents were good to go except this one piece of mail. Now I was supplying it, and I was asking for any exception she would allow. She looked at me without blinking and just shrugged. She told me she couldn't do anything further without the rest of my documentation. I soon realized that by the time I went back to my house and then back to the DMV, I most likely wouldn't have time to complete everything.

I sat in my car and wept. I mean, I really cried ugly. The crying transformed into a complete toddler tantrum with me screaming, "*I don't need this right now! God, seriously! Give me a break!*" I look back now and slightly laugh, because I know how ridiculous I was acting. To be honest, I was immensely hurting, and while this was a pretty big inconvenience, I normally would have never cried hysterically over a situation like this.

The next morning was my birthday, and all I wanted for my birthday at this point was to get my license and not have to go back to the DMV for a very long time. Things were looking up after the lady at the front desk told me that I had all the documents I needed. Now I just had to wait another 2 hours to speak to someone else about the renewal.

It was finally my turn. I took the eye exam and written exam and passed. I thought the guy was about to print my license, and he told me that since my card was expiring that day, I needed to re-take the driving portion. Although I was an emotional wreck, I tried to look as confident as possible, so that they wouldn't try to reschedule the exam.

I was doing so well, and then the driving instructor asked me to parallel park. Although it wasn't my favorite activity, I had parked that way in the past. So I took a deep breath and slowly maneuvered my way into the empty spot. Then the instructor abruptly said, "*Stop the car. Put it in park and give me the keys. You didn't pass.*" My eyes were huge, and I asked, "*Why?*" (which is probably not good to ask, now that I'm thinking about it). She told me that I lightly bumped the orange cone, aka what could have been a child, so I didn't pass. I didn't say it out loud, but I thought, *Well, it could have also just been an orange cone in the road, which would have been fine to lightly bump.* Birthday wish denied. I digress.

I had to return to the DMV the next day with no license. Fast forward to the driving exam. I was doing well, and I don't think I hit any orange cones that time. Actually, I do think I hit one cone, but I'm positive that the driving instructor looked at her phone at that very moment. I started explaining my DMV experience to her, like she was my all of the sudden DMV/life counselor. We were in a neighborhood, and as she began speaking encouraging words to me,

I started to put my foot on the brake pedal while looking at and listening to her. I remember she stopped in the middle of her sentence and said, *"Well, you have to keep driving as I talk to you"*. Right. Of course. When I pulled back to the spot where the exam began, I just knew there was no way she was going to pass me. I mean, I was basically stopped in the middle of the road in a neighborhood for absolutely no reason.

She said, "I'm going to pass you, because I have been dealing with Spring Breakers all week. It was nice not having to deal with a teenager. Plus, I know this has been an extremely hard week for you". I know it was probably inappropriate, but I hugged her with my seat belt still on. I wanted to hug her family and ancestors as well. I could not have been more elated.

Some of you may be wondering why I told you that story. What does my trip to the DMV have to do with Jesus talking to a Samaritan woman at a well? First, will some of you agree that this DMV experience felt like arrows from the pits of hell? It wasn't though in hindsight. I thought I needed a license, and that was it. The Samaritan thought she only needed water from the well, but what we both learned was that we needed a word. I'll be honest, if I would have gotten my license on my birthday, I would have been so happy and grateful, but I would have thought it happened because of what I did. The driving instructor I met was only working two days a week, and I wouldn't have had the opportunity to meet her had I gotten my license the day before I did. Some of you may be saying, *"So what?! At least you got your license, and you didn't have to go back to the DMV!"* Here's the thing. I was happy that I got my license regardless; however, her words about loss and hurt planted a seed of healing. The burden I had been carrying for those few days lightened a little.

It's easy to get caught up in the tasks and if they get completed. God does want us to accomplish certain milestones, which may involve tedious tasks. But most of the time, He is more concerned about our anguished heart. He is more concerned about the interactions we have with one another. He is more concerned about your spiritual health.

Now, I could have avoided this whole situation if I were better at paying attention to the expiration date on my I.D. card. But that is where free will comes into play. When we make decisions and priorities, God may interrupt and say, *"No, you need to be doing this*". Why did I need to go to the DMV 4 times in a week? Why couldn't they just help a broken sister out and give me a new license? How many times did the woman go to the well before encountering Jesus? He needs a receptive heart, and I don't know too much about her story and where she was emotionally on that day, but I do know that the day after my birthday was a desperate day. I had three unsuccessful attempts under my belt, and I was willing to hear from any guidance I could get.

God does not tease nor taunt us. He does not create stressful situations, because we choose our responses. What some people find stressful, others may adapt better. He showed me a side of myself I didn't know was there, a very angry and ugly side. I'll never know if this is true, but I sometimes wonder that if I wouldn't have let that anger out alone in my car in the DMV parking lot, where would it have surfaced otherwise? It wasn't specifically about the DMV, although it may have looked like it was on the surface. This response was a result of a very sad woman dealing with an extremely stressful and time-consuming situation with a total lack of control, slamming into my breaking point.

Later on in the fourth chapter of John, the woman tells Jesus, *"Please, sir, give me this water! Then I'll never be thirsty again, and I won't have to come here to get water"*. Like her lack of excitement regarding her trips to the well, I had the same level of excitement during my trips to the DMV. Yet, what Jesus was offering her was nothing tangible. We like tangible though, don't we? Especially when we are interrupted, we like the result to be something tangible, so we can show the worth of our interruption. However, He doesn't offer her physical water, but rather eternal life. Along with that eternal life, he was asking her to surrender: surrendering all pain, hurt, and sin. This part is for another chapter, but I do want to touch on this for a second. In order to hear clearly from God, I needed to let go of my anger and my voice. He wasn't going to talk over me. Then He used someone to speak to me when my focus was on the road ahead of me (literally and analogically) rather than internally, so I would have a more receptive heart. He knew exactly when I needed to be interrupted for a heart check.

Reflection Time:

Think about your daily routine. Now think about the most recent interruption in your life. If it's easier, write it down. Express your feelings; explain what happened through your perspective, and think about your response.

Now, get real with God about this interruption. Rather than asking Him why He allowed such a thing to happen to you, regardless of it being big or small, ask Him what you can learn from this. Ask Him to give you guidance and wisdom, and most of all, an open heart to hear what He is telling you. Be warned that you may not like the answer, because if it was there to grow you, remember that time under tension and growing pains hurt. They aren't fun, but they can be very beneficial. Ask Him how you can give Him glory through this experience, even if it's by helping someone who also experienced a similar tragedy.

The most important part of this challenge is to take your time. Don't rush to the next chapter just so you can be on the next chapter. God always wants to connect with you. Allow this opportunity for the two of you to connect on a deeper level. Ask Him what word you need to hear, whether it be straight from scripture or a summary of His word through a loved one or stranger. Be open to all opportunities, because if He interrupted you, it was on purpose out of love. He didn't do it to mess with you or punish you. He interrupted you, because He wants to help you through something. But to be helped, you have to look to Him; otherwise, your gaze will be somewhere else.

Breaking Barriers

The woman was surprised, for Jews refused to have anything to do with Samaritans. She said to Jesus, "You are a Jew, and I am a Samaritan woman. Why are you asking me for a drink?" (John 4:9)

The timing of her arrival to the well adds another dimension to this passage. Local residents would go to the well to collect water and to socialize/gossip. To avoid the judgment and possible harassment, the Samaritan woman would go to Jacob's Well during the hottest times of the day when she knew no one else would be there. The Word says that she was carrying a jar to collect water. This was not like a cute mason jar. For efficiency purposes, she was carrying quite a large jar, so that she wouldn't have to make 100 trips a day to the well. I can't even imagine the weight she was carrying before and after the water. On top of that, the heat was at its highest degree of the day when she arrived. She was willing to risk her physical health just so she wouldn't have to approach a certain group, or maybe it was one specific person.

Sometimes all it takes is a hurtful look from someone to crush another's spirit. Maybe she was negatively approached by one of the local residents or even a group. Maybe a friend didn't take up for her when she was being judged by others. Maybe she was told that she was too dysfunctional to spend time with, because she's been married too many times. Maybe she was seen as unstable by others, and instead of someone sticking by her side and praying with her during the good and bad days, they pushed her away. Maybe she saw the space slowly being created by groups of people, and she took the liberty of completing that separation by no longer attending at the same time she knew the others would be at the well. Maybe someone put a spirit of fear in her, approached her in a forceful way because of her marriage history, and now she is trying to find control in everything she does. Maybe now she always looks over her shoulder, wondering if someone will see her and hurt her again. While all or none of these maybes could have been the case for her, just one can be enough to give someone the excuse to question validation and begin the process of isolation.

Isolation doesn't necessarily mean that you aren't seen. People may see your face, but it is only a version of you. Social media has caused an epidemic of isolation with people all over the world. Not only do we have our faces buried in our phones when we are surrounded by others, but we layer filters on our pictures to not be fully seen. Lord forbid anyone sees a flaw. There is no way anyone should know that you have a vulnerable side. Now I am not saying to go on a full blown vent rampage on social media and let everyone know every thought you've had since your sixth birthday. I am saying that it's ok to not be perfect, and that putting a cover on what you think is a flaw may be something someone else needs to see in order to be healed.

Satan had that woman thinking that she needed to hide from others, giving her spirits of fear, hopelessness, and unworthiness. After only one conversation with the Savior of the world, she rushes to a crowd, hoping to gather as many people as possible to share her experience. What she was trying to hide (herself) was now the center of attention. While it would have been an amazing miracle for a

Jewish man to be healed, Jesus brought it to a whole new level when He brought healing to a woman who everyone rejected, neglected, avoided, and judged.

Most of the time, isolation is caused by not meeting someone else's timeline regarding our lives and all the pressure that comes along with it, so we avoid more and more people to keep from feeling a sense of failure. Have you ever isolated yourself? Isolation can cause us to make some irrational decisions due to fear. It doesn't necessarily mean that you are sitting alone in your living room. Nowadays there is a phrase called *FOMO*, and it means the Fear of Missing Out. Another popular word is *clout*, and that simply means someone worth following. Social media makes us think we are trend setters and leaders, but really we are all followers. Isolation is the result of a constant comparison game that is played until it narrows down the group to one person. Even though the person may be successful in many areas of life, that one section where they fall short can cause stress and even fear.

As I pondered on why this woman went to the well at such a hot hour of the day, I could understand why some people may think that's a little ridiculous; however, I could completely relate. I went through a serious period of isolation about 3 years ago, and I didn't see a way of stopping. People around me tried to help, and when I didn't respond to their advice as quickly as they wanted me to, frustration would occur. It's not that I wanted to isolate myself. I was living in a state of fear and anger, and nothing would change until those chains were broken in my life.

Because of the negativity in my heart, I was a negative person on the outside. I tried so hard to wear the mask that showed the fake smile. I forced the laughter at times, just so people around me wouldn't judge the depression. I thought if I acted like a certain person, it would be good enough, but none of it was real. The whole thing was a production for years. I was faking my smile so much that I was even able to fool myself into thinking I was happy. I know that may sound strange, but it is true. We are able to fool ourselves when we don't know our full worth. My life turned into a concept: *This will do for now.* Have you ever settled for less than you deserve? Whether it be a paycheck, a relationship, a diagnosis, or anything negative spoken over your life, did you allow yourself to believe a mediocre truth for your future for any length of time? Are you experiencing that feeling now?

My healing came in stages. I had friends and family members talking to Jesus on my behalf for a long time before I spoke to Him. Things change when you talk to Jesus.

When Jesus was at the well, His disciples (who weren't with Him at the time), were under the impression that He was only here for the Jews. Also, Jewish people and Samaritans didn't converse. Samaria was known for its wild parties and intense debauchery. Enter Jesus. Not only does He speak to a Samaritan, but He spoke to a Samaritan woman, which was NOT something any Jewish man would ever be seen doing. Not only did He speak to a Samaritan woman, but He offered her everlasting life by using the water analogy, which was showing her and everyone who read this part of the Book of John, that Jesus came to save us all. There is no such thing as a "Jesus type". There is no form with checkboxes that qualifies anyone to be able to have a conversation with Him. In fact, it is more likely that Jesus will speak to the person without the Bible in his/her hand before He would walk up to the Christian.

We are beautifully broken. It's in those broken pieces where the Holy Spirit flows through us and fills those holes that we cannot fill. When we are always put together, we are not giving room for

God to move in us. When we bring our brokenness to Him, He not only glues those pieces back together, but He makes us brand new. Healing doesn't always come with forgetfulness. Instead it comes with grace and mercy. He gives us memory for safety, so that we won't keep making the same mistakes and/or getting hurt in the same ways.

Maybe in your waiting, you want a relationship with Christ, but you feel like you don't meet the requirements. Maybe you've experienced some religious judgment and isolation from churches, but you still find yourself needing Christ. I want to encourage you that He will always help His lost sheep, because that's why He came to the world in the first place. The religious people who are throwing condemnation and harsh judgements are not representing Christ. Don't be confused. However, He does want you to seek Him. There may be tests of your faith, but your persistence and obedience will be seen and acknowledged by God. Always. Don't let others talk you into drifting away from God, because society tells you that you don't fit the mold of what a Christian looks like. By acknowledging Him as your Savior and following Him, leaving your past in the past, you are His child and He loves you unconditionally. He doesn't need time to warm up to you. There is nothing you can think, say, or do that will make Jesus turn away from you forever. He will always answer when you call. Don't listen to anyone who is telling you that you aren't good enough. Let His voice be the only voice you hear. May your Father's lullaby be forever in your heart.

If you are like me, there has been a time (maybe more than once) in your life when you didn't feel worthy to talk to God. Maybe that time is now. You may feel anger, shame, guilt, distrust, frustration, betrayal, neglect, or a number of other negative emotions. Maybe it has nothing to do with emotion. Maybe you feel like you don't necessarily look like a Christian, because you see others in church who look and act differently from you. Maybe someone even told you that you don't fit into Christianity because of your past or present. Jesus annihilated this concept through this short, but deep conversation with a woman that many people would have thought should have never happened. We later learn that because this conversation happened, hundreds of people accepted Christ into their hearts.

What shook me the most was that He arrived before her. He was waiting on her. She didn't have to seek Him. He was already there for her. This woman was going through the motions of life, making some unhealthy decisions, and feeling weights that were never hers to bear. Jesus met her, knowing that pain she was fighting internally and freely offered to take it from her. Regardless of what anyone else thought or said, Jesus reached out to her, not condemning her, but fighting for her.

You don't have to live in your past for the rest of your life. He wants you to have a bright and amazing future. He created this life for you to love and learn, not to suffer through and adapt. He is with us through it all, and He knew every step you would ever take, every conversation you would ever have, every decision you would ever make, every laugh and tear you would ever experience. He knows every detail of your life, including every hair on your head. He knows all this, because He created you. He knows that life can get really hard. Jesus knows what betrayal feels like; He knows neglect. He knows what it feels like to be mocked, abused, and wrongly accused. He understands physical, emotional, and mental pain. There is nothing that you could bring to Him where He wouldn't have experienced this, too. He is within us. He experiences everything we experience. Although He tells us not to go in certain directions, He never leaves us at the crossroad; He goes freely with us, never abandoning us. Although it can feel like a terrifying road, He is creating a path always for us to escape to His presence. We have to lean into that. We need to know He does want us. You are wanted. You are needed. You are loved.

Reflection Time:

When you look in the mirror, how do you respond? When you receive a compliment, how do you respond? Pay attention to your words, actions, and thoughts. Are you putting labels on yourself? Where are those labels stemming from? Did someone once tell you that you weren't smart enough, pretty enough, talented enough, good enough, and now it has become your identity? Does how you speak about yourself align with how God speaks of you? If you think that God has anything negative to say about you, you need to go back into the Word. He always has and always will speak love and light over your life. In His Word, He shows the immense interest of your existence, not only by knowing how many hairs are on your head, but by innocently and freely sacrificing His life for you. Knowing you were the reason for His crucifixion, He still lovingly prayed for you, that you would be forgiven for any and all sins. He took all of it and captured it on the cross.

Discernment & Godly Counsel

Jesus replied, "If you only knew the gift God has for you and who you are speaking to, you would ask Me, and I would give you living water".

"But sir, you don't have a rope or a bucket," she said, "and this well is very deep. Where would you get this living water? And besides do you think you're greater than our ancestor, Jacob, who gave us this well? How can you offer better water than he and his sons and his animals enjoyed?"

Jesus replied, "Anyone who drinks this water will soon become thirsty again. But those who drink the water I give will never be thirsty again. It becomes a fresh, bubbling spring within them, giving them eternal life". (John 4:10-14)

It makes me laugh when I read her response in this section. She is asking Jesus if He thinks He is better than their ancestors, referring to Jacob and his sons. Let's reflect on who she is talking about. Who is Jacob? Who are Jacob's sons? Well, Joseph is one of Jacob's sons. Joseph, the husband of Mary, had a big test of humility when He found out that his wife conceived a child without him participating. On an Earthly stage, Jacob is Jesus's grandfather, and one of his sons is Jesus's Earthly father. All that being said, Jesus didn't give her that back story. He didn't explain all the intimate details of his slightly dramatic childhood. He went back to the theme of the conversation, disregarding the woman's somewhat condescending question, and explained that she will have a much better quality of life if she takes what He is offering to her.

Just as a side note, when you are speaking with someone about something, and they come back at you with slight aggravation or a negative attitude, do not feed into it. Do not give away so many details about your side that it turns into an unofficial courtroom. You don't need to participate in an argument just because the opportunity presents itself. Stay focused the main topic, and once it is said, be done with it. Jesus easily could have laughed in her face, explaining the ancestors would be nothing without Him; however, He didn't for her sake and for the respect of the lineage. It all had a purpose, and all of it was good. Jesus teaches humility and patience here.

He is also teaching about godly counsel. Let me explain. What this woman didn't realize was that she was hearing what she needed to hear; however, she wasn't listening. She was too caught up in her mind. Jesus was showing her that her waiting period could end if she simply listened to Him. Many times we seek God's Word during the waiting periods, but scripture doesn't always make sense. You may find yourself reading over and over and wondering how you can relate to what you're reading. You may even get to a point where you give up on God's Word, because what He's saying to you through His Word is not being interpreted correctly.

Notice that the Samaritan woman did not immediately understand what Jesus was telling her, because she wasn't willing to open her mind and reach out to the right resource, which for her was Jesus standing right in front of her.

It wasn't just the woman who Jesus used to teach about godly counsel. His disciples, men who had been by his side for years and told of how God uses the unlikely person, still inaudibly questioned Jesus's actions when they found the two at the well. This goes to show you that interpretation of the Word matters, especially since these men were being trained to spread the news of the Gospel.

The waiting period is given to you by God to develop and gain wisdom, but we must open our minds and hearts for this to work. God puts people, scenarios, and atmospheres constantly in front of us to show us what we need to see and hear what we need to hear, but we need to pray for an open heart and mind to be able to embrace all that God has for us.

Although the two were speaking the same language, the woman interpreted Jesus with a completely different meaning. If she wouldn't have asked what He meant, she would have remained confused and possibly shared the wrong truth with another person. There are a number of places in the Bible where someone who is reading it for the first time or the first time in a long time could get a little confused. This is why I highly advise that you always seek godly counsel with the Word.

This is probably my favorite topic, because I think a lot of people can relate to this one. I'll use an analogy. Have you ever gone to the gym, looked at all the equipment with no idea what it was made for, yet tried it anyway? You could have asked for help, but you didn't want to embarrass yourself, yet at the same time willing to fracture, sprain, or break a ligament from not knowing if this contraption is a leg raiser or arm curler. The same can be said about church. So many of us go to church to be healed, but we don't engage ourselves in the church. Many of us don't seek counsel from the heads of the church. Maybe you have, but something didn't sound right. Seeking godly counsel is so important. I know this may not be what you want to hear, but you need help. You may be able to do most of what you want, but eventually you will need help. That is where mentors come in. God did not create us to do life alone. Never be ashamed to ask. Have you ever said, *"I love God and trust Him, but I still feel very sad"*? It's because you are trying to do everything on your own.

Now if she were to ask someone in Samaria about this, she would get a biased answer just as much as she would from a Jewish leader, but she asked Jesus who holds the truth. We may not have the opportunity to look Jesus in the eyes and ask Him questions like she did. That's why it's so important to know God's Word before you speak to someone, because it closes gaps in the conversation that could lead you on a destructive path. Don't put the responsibility of your entire life on one person's counsel. Also, don't seek those who will only agree with you. Know that you don't know everything and always have room to grow. Accept that you may have to make some serious changes in your life, and be prepared for any possibility.

Also, when you start aligning your life with God's Will, satan's ears pop up. He will begin to try to stop you in any way he can. If you feel like your life is going by pretty easily, that usually means satan doesn't feel threatened by you at all. That's not a good thing. I'm not saying that you have to live in utter turmoil at all times as a Christian, but you will have a jealous enemy who is extremely annoying and adamant on stopping you from bringing glory to God. He's ridiculous and knows all your weak spots, so lift those up to God and ask the Holy Spirit to fill the gaps on your behalf. Even highly successful, independent people, like yourself, need help from God. Leave your pride at the door, and ask God for a hedge of protection over you and all of your friends and families.

Reflection Time:

Who do you go to for spiritual guidance? Does any of the advice you receive differ from what the Bible says? Is there anything you are currently experiencing that you prefer to do on your own? If so, what is it? Are you willing to seek help from others, or do you need time?

Surrendering All

"Please, sir," the woman said, "give me this water! Then I'll never be thirsty again, and I won't have to come here to get water".

"Go and get your husband," Jesus told her.

"I don't have a husband," the woman replied.

Jesus said, "You're right! You don't have a husband---for you have had five husbands, and you aren't even married to the man you are living with now. You certainly spoke the truth!" (John 4:15-18)

This may sound like Jesus is condemning the woman for her lifestyle, but that is not happening at all. In fact, without saying, Jesus is referencing more than just the woman's relationship status. When she asked Jesus for the Living Water, she was asking for her salvation without even realizing it. Jesus was showing her that when you receive the Living Water, we must bring everything to Him, surrendering all our most prized possessions and make Him our greatest priority.

This conversation does kickstart a thought process of how often we pray for people in our lives, the roles we give them, and if those roles align with God's Word and His intentions. When we ask for Living Water, we need to be able to bring everything to Jesus's feet, all of our mess. There may be some things that you are embarrassed by, but God already knows about that. There's nothing you can do, say, or think that will shock Him.

We live in a very spiritual world, and most of what we deal with, whether it be from our free will or attacks from the devil, are spirits that need to be broken from our lives. They will find a host in us and make us think that life is supposed to feel a certain way all the time, but that is wrong. That is why Jesus asked the Samaritan woman to bring her boyfriend to Him, cleansing them from acts of sin with one another. By her doing this, she is giving Jesus all parts of her life. He doesn't want us to keep nor hide any part of ourselves from Him. Jesus will meet you in love and will heal this spirit of shame and all other sinful nature in your life when you bring it to Him in obedience.

Just as a side note, make sure that all your intentions are to glorify God. If you are praying for the man you're sleeping with to surrender to God, there could be a small chance that he is so fixated on your body that he doesn't see the Body of Christ. Surrendering all your relationships to God is truly the best benefit, because you will never have what you fully deserve without your full surrender.

Reflection Time:

Think of all your relationships. What role have you given each person? I don't just mean family member names; I also mean, do you allow certain people to be the voice of reason for you in certain areas vs others? What type of influences do you allow? Do you have any toxic relationships? Are you engaging in any sinful relationships? Have YOU talked to Jesus about all of your relationships?

Don't be afraid to speak to Jesus about your relationships. I know you may disagree now, but if He takes someone out of your life, it's because He loves you. I don't mean in the sense of losing someone and dealing with grief. I am talking more about two people going their separate ways to grow into better people. When people you love, yet are unhealthy for you to be around, are no longer around, trust that some people are only here for seasons. Maybe you were the blessing for that person. While the experience could have been horrible for you, maybe God used you without you even knowing to build that other person into who He needed the other person to be. This is just my opinion, but I don't believe anyone is introduced to you by accident; however, I do believe God has intentions on those relationships, and it is not our jobs to persuade God to think otherwise. I promise He knows better than you.

Prayer Life

"Sir," the woman said, "you must be a prophet. So tell me, why is it that you Jews insist that Jerusalem is the only place of worship, while we Samaritans claim it is here at Mount Gerizim, where our ancestors worshipped?"

Jesus replied, "Believe me, dear woman, the time is coming when it will no longer matter whether you worship the Father on the mountain or in Jerusalem. You Samaritans know very little about the One you worship, while we Jews know all about Him, for salvation comes through the Jews. But the time is coming---indeed it's here now---when true worshipers will worship the Father in spirit and in truth. The Father is looking for those who will worship Him that way. For God is Spirit, so those who worship Him must worship in spirit and in truth." (John 4:19-24)

Let's break apart this scripture a little, first looking at what and how the Samaritan woman spoke and then Jesus's response and meaning. The woman asked Jesus where she should pray in order to be best heard from God. Without openly asking, she is basically looking in Jesus's eyes and questioning, *"How can I get a guarantee that I will have my prayers answered?"* She is focusing on ritual and tradition, which makes total sense, because that's all she's ever known. She is also somewhat using a bargaining tactic by unofficially asking, *"If I do this, will God do this?"* That's one thing you should never do. Never bargain with God.

I'll give you a relatable scenario. Let's pretend you are going through a break-up, and you want that person to come back into your life and be with you forever. Knowing it was not a healthy relationship, you still pray to God that He brings that person back in your life and creates a deep and long-lasting love. When He says, *"No"*, then you start saying you'll do all these things to please Him. You will give up things. You will read His Word more. You will pray more. The list goes on and on. Don't you think God sees through you? If you aren't doing those now, why would He believe that you will start doing those things with a greater distraction in your life, like the person from your previously toxic relationship? Also, don't you think that's a little cringe-worthy on a certain level? You're basically showing Him conditional love, which is heart-breaking to the One who gives us unconditional love on a second to second basis.

Jesus wiped that concept clean, giving her no opportunity to bargain, because He said that it doesn't matter where you pray anymore. The location of your body does not depend on if God listens or not. He is more concerned with the location of your heart, not physically, but spiritually. In other words, do you have faith? Faith forces us to release our will and surrender to His, with no tangible answer most of the time. There's no checkbox that says, "*I prayed on the mountain top, so God will answer this prayer the way I want Him to now*". The way that Jesus explains prayer is that He is not a genie. It is all about our spirits aligning with God's Will.

Additionally, when Jesus said that salvation comes through the Jews, He is referencing Himself more than the current Jewish community. He is referring to the lineage that God has intricately planned since day 1.

This is the hardest chapter for me to write, because like the woman at the well, I asked God how I should pray in order to be heard, not for wisdom but for self-gain. During the most desperate days of my life, I found myself bargaining with God, which meant I clearly did not understand grace and faith.

Praying can be quite a romantic concept, but on a long-term scale, prayers require faith. The first time you pray about something, you will most likely have the most positive energy; however, as time passes, the true test of faith happens. Let's use a workout regimen as an example. When we decide to begin a workout program, maybe you print out a planned calendar, buy only produce at the grocery store, pick out that pair of pants you are determined to fit into by the end (whatever that means to you), and start making short-term and long-term plans. We think about the perfectly chiseled bodies we will have in only 2 weeks, and life will be so lovely. A similar situation can be said with our prayer lives. Some of us may think that when we accept Christ, our prayers will cut in line to reach God quicker. We will now be protected from all hurt and pain, and life will be bliss. But then the soreness from so many workouts set in. Maybe you don't get enough rest the night before, or you are craving ice cream instead of a quinoa salad. You don't see the results, and you wonder if this is the right program for you. Yet, you look at your trainer and realize this person has to know what he/she is talking about.

What you need to remember is that person put in quite a few more hours/days/months/years than you have. You have to push further than your feelings. So when it comes to trusting God and giving your prayer life to Him, know that you won't always be smiling. It's so custom for us to blame and question God when tragedy strikes. Remember that many times when we blame God, it is not God at all. Sometimes it's satan, who comes to steal, kill, and destroy. Other times it's us. God gave us free will, and even though He allowed you to meet a human being doesn't mean it was ever His intention for you two to date. Now your heart is broken, and you're asking God, "*Why?*" Maybe God is saying, "*I didn't tell you to date him/her. In fact, I showed you so many red flags, and you just covered your eyes*". Maybe the reason we don't hear and see God is because we have our hands over our eyes and ears. This, my friends, may be where we start our journey of faith.

Sister, one thing I learned over the last couple years is that God answers every prayer, but free will is SUPER free. I mean, more than I realized. If you think that God blessed you with something that is going to keep you strapped for money or sacrificing your beliefs, you aren't listening well enough. He is not a God who only gives a percentage of the blessing. He goes all in.

When you pray, pray for God's Will, not your will. Pray for God's Will, not your will. One more time. Pray for God's Will, not your will. You may think that there is a pause in your life, but your prayer is not a pause; it's a seed, and seeds grow. Wait patiently for that harvest, and recognize that this seed is God's seed and not your seed. The plant may look different than you planned, but when it's from God, it is good. *"But what if he doesn't come back to me?"* It is good. *"What if we don't end up together?"* It is good. *"What if I have to be single for a long time?"* It is good. You know why? Because God's Will is always good. The same can be said for our married ladies or those in relationships. Maybe you're praying to have a better relationship with your children, and everyday feels more and more like a challenge. Maybe there is some financial tension between you and your spouse, and you aren't seeing any way out. Do the opposite of what you feel. Stand in agreement with your spouse that God is good. He always has been, and He always will be.

Goodness doesn't always feel good. Goodness may feel more like stretching and growing, like the stem coming out of a seed or loosening the lactic acid in your muscles through yoga. But when you are being stretched, you are growing. If you are not growing, you are dying. When God stands over your life, He said I'll take the weight, if you give me the glory.

God wants us to pray about every single relationship in our lives. This is not only for romantic relationships. In order to have the most fulfilling relationships in all areas of life, Jesus wants us to bring every single encounter to Him. If you started at a new job, He wants you to lift up every single person you work with. He wants you to discuss relations with new friends, new organizations, all of them. Every single person who enters your life, God wants to discuss this with you. The reason is that He wants you to hear Him if He is giving you red flags. If you don't talk to Him about it, you may not be looking for what you need to be looking for.

In life, you will meet a lot of nice people. Now I need to be blunt with you. Do not pour your heart into that person if they do not have a faith-filled foundation. I don't mean this in a judgmental way. A lot of times when trials hit, people with faith act much differently than people who do not practice a faith-filled life. The ones who don't have a deep faith may "not know what to say to you." They may leave you alone, because you are making that person depressed. They may explode and yell at you, and/or turn to alcohol, drugs, and other people who can make them smile. If they are only focused on smiling, and they disappear during the hard times, don't pour into those people. You want someone who is on his/her knees alongside you, hand on your shoulder, fervently praying for and with you, believing God can move mountains. This person will check on you and speak life to you.

You may want to be at a club rather than a church, because there are more people and less guilt. Here's the thing: The club may seem crowded, but no one is there for you. They are only there to have a good time. Smiling is great and all, but unless you have a numb face, your cheeks will get sore if you smile for too long. Once that smile is gone, and it's just two faces, what is there? What substance is there? Is the only substance you have in common substance abuse? Instead of looking for a quick solution (that will more than likely give you another set of problems), trust God's timing and His Word through it all.

Fight your battles with your hands lifted in surrender. When it looks like a good thing is coming your way, don't drop your hands. Keep surrendering to Him. Pray about every single encounter. Ask the Holy Spirit to guide you in this relationship. Don't take the lead with any relationship, for it was God who put that person in front of you. Ask Him what He needs from you for this person. He loves you and wants to give you an abundance, but remember that all the glory goes to Him. He wants to make you smile, but He never wants you to think the smile came from anyone other than Him. No matter who is standing in front of you, remember that person has a Creator. The Creator is who made you smile. The Creator is the one who blessed you with a gift today. The Creator is who is building something exceptional with the two of you. All He asks of you is to surrender. Throw away your will and control. Get rid of ungodly influences. Praise Him in all of it.

1 Corinthians says that *"Love is patient"*. That being said, when you are wondering where God is and begging Him to come through to you, know that He is being patient with you. He is with you, but He is patiently waiting for you to be ready for His blessing. Part of that readiness is letting go of earthly desires, including

people, places, and things. He is patiently waiting for our spiritual cleanse. It's not that God is less mighty and can't work. He is being patient for your sake, so that you can experience the greatness of God without being distracted by those things you have yet surrendered. He wants you to have a life that's more than mediocre. Know that God is not a God of mediocrity; so if you are praying for financial freedom, and you get an unexpected $10 check in the mail, know that's just the beginning of God's grace in your life. Ten dollars is not all God can do. Maybe He only allowed that little kiss from heaven because He is working on your actions. He wants you to learn budgeting, and He does not spoil His children to the point where they treat Him as a genie. He wants us to always rely on Him, but He wants us to be wise with how He blesses us.

You may be praying for an amazing man in your life, but you yell at everyone in your family. Maybe He is working on your anger before He brings that blessing. Ask the Holy Spirit to reveal what needs to be revealed in your heart for Him to complete a mighty work in you. You know that He can do big things in your life, so a big blessing is not about His capabilities. It's about how you receive them. Receive the blessings with gratitude and bring glory to God always.

Sometimes we question where God is when times are hard, and prayers seem unanswered. When we ask God where He is and why He didn't do what we asked Him to do, God's Word implies that we are confusing His love with our agendas. This goes back to when Jesus tells her to *"worship in spirit and in truth"*. There was a reason He added, *"in truth"*. There are spirits that can disguise themselves to cause confusion and destruction in your life. So when you pray, it is important that your spirit is rooted in His Truth. If it is, you can trust that the result will always be good in time.

Reflection Time:
Write down five areas of your life that you tend to keep control and not allow God to completely take care of it. It may be your finances, your children, your marriage, or even your diet. By writing all of them down, you can have a visual of some strongholds in your life that need to be broken. What areas of your life do you need to leave your jar? After writing them down, I want you to pray about each one individually. Ask God for forgiveness and ask in the Name of Jesus that these strongholds are permanently severed from

your spirit. Then ask the Holy Spirit to fill this newly empty part of you with grace, love, and protection.

Leaving Your Jar

The woman said, "I know the Messiah is coming—the one who is called Christ. When He comes, He will explain everything to us". Then Jesus told her, "I AM the Messiah!" Just then his disciples came back. They were shocked to find him talking to a woman, but none of them had the nerve to ask, "What do you want with her?" or "Why are you talking to her?" The woman left her water jar beside the well and ran back to the village, telling everyone, "Come and see a man who told me everything I ever did! Could He possibly be the Messiah?" So the the people came streaming from the village to see Him.

Meanwhile, the disciples were urging Jesus, "Rabbi, eat something". But Jesus replied, "I have a kind of food you know nothing about". "Did someone bring Him food while we were gone?" the disciples asked each other.

Then Jesus explained: "My nourishment comes from doing the will of God, who sent Me, and from finishing His work. You know the saying, Four months between planting and harvest. But I say, wake up and look around. The fields are already ripe for harvest. The harvesters are paid good wages, and the fruit they harvest is people brought to eternal life. What joys awaits both the planter and the harvester alike! You know the saying, One plants and another harvests. And it's true. I sent you to harvest where you didn't plant; others had already done the work, and now you will get to gather the harvest".

Many Samaritans from the village believed in Jesus because the woman had said, "He told me everything I ever did!" When they came out to see Him, they begged Him to stay in their village. So He stayed for two days, long enough for many more to hear His message and believe. Then they said to the woman, "Now we believe, not just because of what you told us, but because we have heard Him ourselves. Now we know that He is indeed the Savior of the world". (John 4:25-42)

As I read this passage in the Book of John, it gave me chills, because it showed me how God uses us as vessels. It is not our job to completely convert people's hearts; only God can do that. It is our job, however, to plant that seed. It is our job to share His story, and then God will take over the rest for us. He will lead others in the way He intends them to be led. We cannot and should not force a belief system on anyone. All we can and should do is to share His story and how good He is in our lives, and let that seed be planted and watered by so many other experiences. Trust that when God allows you to plant a spiritual seed within someone's heart, it is not necessarily your job to stick around to make sure it is being watered. Believe that if God can bring your word to that person's ears, He is fully capable of continuing to bring the right people in that person's life to experience the fullness of God.

He has called us to be the salt of the Earth and light of the world, and the Samaritan woman is a prime example of this. Matthew 5:13-14 says, *"You are the salt of the Earth. But what good is salt if it has lost its flavor? Can you make it salty again? It will be thrown out and trampled underfoot as worthless. You are the light of the world---like a city on a hilltop that cannot be hidden. No one lights a lamp and then puts it under a basket. Instead, a lamp is placed on a stand, where it gives light to everyone in the house. In the same way, let your good deeds shine out for all to see, so that everyone will praise your heavenly Father"*.

Don't lose the flavor of God. I'm from Louisiana, and we are all about our seasoning. If you took away seasoning from my meals, I would be so disappointed and not be able to enjoy the food as much as I would prefer, nor would I want to share with anyone. However, if I had seasoning, then I wouldn't be able to eat the food fast enough. When we talk about God, we don't want to have a bland conversation. God is full of flavor, and our individuality is a source He uses for His good, to help lighten the path for others on dark days.

Maybe you are more like a villager right now, and this is the first time you're learning about who God is. I can talk to you all day about all the great things God has done in my life, but that is not all you need to experience the maximum potential of God's love for you. Go directly to Him with your words and ears. Talk to Him; be real with Him. Tell Him if you are happy, stressed out, confused, angry, lost, and/or anything you are going through and thinking. Share it all, but make sure you give Him time as well. Read His Word, and let Him speak to you. Clothe yourself with the promises He gives you throughout scripture. Sit in silence, close your eyes, and ask the Holy Spirit to speak to you. With that, go to someone who is a Bible-based Christian who will give you sound advice on what the next steps are.

While reading about a redemption story is always a great way to have encouragement and motivation, it's important to realize that with every story, there is unspoken resistance. It's not all about the end result. So when you are going through your journey, and resistance meets you (because it will), it's important that you keep godly counsel close, as stated in a previous chapter. If you only let yourself focus on the redemption story endings, you will feel like you got sucker-punched when things get a little complicated. You may create a comparison game in your head unintentionally, which can be extremely destructive if you don't control how far you let it go.

To go full circle from mass healing to waiting on a woman, we see in the Word that Jesus went to the well to rest, but we know by now that Jesus never rests. Even when He is still, He is still moving. Even though He was in a grave, He was still working. There was never a second of the day that He wasn't creating a new promise for each one of us. Even though He may not have been visible to some of the people seeking Him, He was still working in their lives. Sometimes your healing comes from someone else being healed. Because the woman met with Jesus that day, the Word says that hundreds surrendered to His name because of their encounter.

He wasn't tunnel-visioned with this woman. He saw the bigger picture, but that is how good God is. Even though He is always thinking about every single one of His children and their salvation, He still gives us individual attention every day that we need. He is omnipresent. The battle belongs to Him, not to you. Release control. Give it back to Him. It was never yours to fight.

To me, one of the most powerful parts of this scripture is when it said that the Samaritan woman left her water jar to go and tell others about her experience. For one, she went to the well at an hour when she knew no one would be there; this was so she didn't need to worry about judgement or unwanted gossip from others around her. After meeting Jesus, that fear and shame disappeared, and she rushed to a crowd to create a spiritual harvest. Like Christ, she abandoned her needs for the sake of others. One visit with Christ changed her life forever.

Reflection Time:

So, what will you allow Him to do for you? What will you do for Him?

Printed in Great Britain
by Amazon

17213420R00032